HIP-HOP LEGENDS ALPHABET

Words by Robin Feiner

A is for André 3000.
Hey ya! With his fresh, funky style, this Atlanta rap legend made sure the world knew the South had something to say. As Outkast, 'dré and co-creator Big Boi's "Southernplayalisticadillacmuzik" ushered in a whole new wave of hip-hop.

B is for Notorious **B**.I.G. With his laid-back delivery, Biggie Smalls hypnotized millions. He was the king of East Coast rap, and frequently collaborated with his friend Puff Daddy. Biggie's career tragically ended at 24, but many call Big Poppa the best rapper ever.

C is for **C**huck D.
Chuck D's Public Enemy
helped prove the power of
hip-hop. With strong lyrics
about issues facing the African
American community, Chuck D
was more than an MC. He was
the leader of a movement,
and a socially and politically
conscious legend.

D is for Dr. Dre.
This rap titan came straight outta Compton with funky sounds and slower beats to help create the West Coast style called G-funk in the early '90s. A legend in the booth and on the mic, Dre has produced hits from 2Pac, Eminem, and Snoop Dogg.

E is for **E**minem.
A white rapper from Detroit, the real Slim Shady shattered traditional hip-hop barriers and helped bring rap to the Midwest. Marshall Mathers is known just as well for his controversial lyrics as he is for his famous mic skills.

F is for Foxy Brown. Challenging the male-dominated genre with strong, proud lyrics, Foxy changed the game for female rappers, and became a superstar before age 18. In 1999, her "Chyna Doll" became just the second female rap album to debut atop the Billboard charts.

G is for **G**randmaster Flash. Considered by many to be the OG DJ, his pioneering mixing and scratching techniques were the sonic backbone of Grandmaster Flash and the Furious Five. Many call their song "The Message" the best and most important rap song of all time.

H is for Lauryn Hill.
Her singsong style made
Hill one of hip-hop's most
inspirational voices. This '90s
icon killed them softly with the
Fugees before releasing solo
masterpiece "The Miseducation
of Lauryn Hill" in 1998. It was
the first rap release to win
Album of the Year.

I is for **I**ce Cube.
As part of N.W.A, he helped put West Coast rap on the map in the late '80s. Cube wrote and delivered raw, powerful lyrics that pushed boundaries and explored police brutality and other issues facing boyz n the hood. He then became a movie star.

J is for **J**am Master Jay. This DJ legend and his Run-DMC groupmates spent the '80s taking down sucker MCs and bringing hip-hop to the streets. Providing the unmistakable foundation for the group, Jam Master Jay helped Run-DMC introduce rap to a wider audience.

K is for Lil' Kim.
Don't be fooled by the name — Lil' Kim is a giant of rap who flipped the script, unafraid to show what females could do in a male-dominated genre. In 2006 she became just the second female rapper to have three albums certified platinum.

L is for *MC* **L**yte.
She had the power to eat
you up with a rhyme. MC Lyte
helped lay a platform for
some of rap's most famous
femcees. Her 1988 album
"Lyte as a Feather" was the
first solo release by a female
rapper. A pioneering legend.

M is for **M**issy Elliott.
With an unmistakable style,
this supa dupa fly legend
has been working it on the
mic and in music videos since
launching her solo career in
1997. Missy 'Misdemeanor'
Elliott has sold more than
30 million records and owns
one of the most creative
minds in hip-hop history.

N is for Nas.
This legend's New York state of mind produced some of the most authentic songs about the NYC streets. His 1994 debut "Illmatic" is considered one of the best and most influential rap albums of all time, breathing new life into the Big Apple hip-hop scene.

Oo

**O is for KRS-One.
KRS-One and Boogie Down Productions were pillars of rap in the '80s. While he initially used his free-flowing style to defend the Bronx's claim as the birthplace of hip-hop, KRS-One later shifted his focus to being a Teacha, using his platform for political activism.**

P is for **P**hife Dawg.
A founding member of A Tribe Called Quest, the Five-Foot Assassin was small in stature but huge in influence. Phife and the rest of his Tribe are one of hip-hop's most respected groups, and helped popularize an alternative style that incorporated jazz sounds.

Qq

Q is for **Q**ueen Latifah.
A sister dope enough to
make you holler and scream
always made sure to put ladies
first, preaching U.N.I.T.Y. and
speaking out against the abuse
and unfair treatment women
received in the rap world.
All hail the Queen.

R is for **R**akim.
Real hip-hop heads say Rakim was one of the best to ever do it. "To me, he invented the flow," rap superstar Ice-T said. This legend introduced more complicated rhyming and writing to rap. He and Eric B's "Paid in Full" has been called the best rap album of all time.

S is for **S**alt.
Salt-N-Pepa were hot, cool, vicious, and knew how to push it. The First Ladies of Hip-Hop inspired some of rap's greatest voices. "We're feminists doing something that only guys are expected to do and doin' it right!" Salt said. Spoken like a true legend.

T is for **T**upac Shakur. With the help of Dr. Dre, it was all eyez on 2Pac as he spread his California love across the world, selling more than 75 million records. Sadly, like his East Coast rival the Notorious B.I.G., Pac's career was cut short by tragedy.

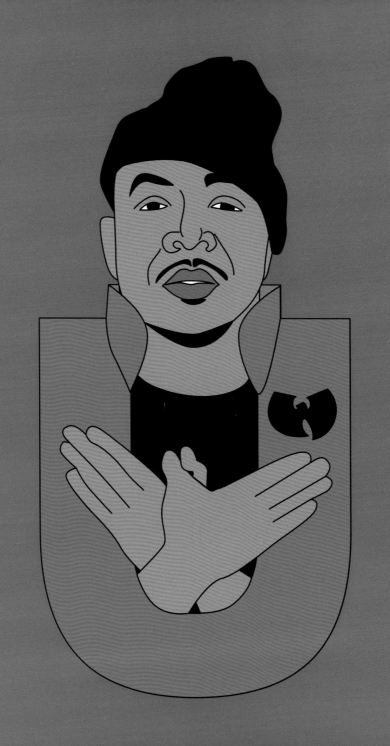

U is for **U-God.**
The four-bar killer was a
member of perhaps the best
rap group ever, Wu-Tang Clan.
His rough rapping style mixed
perfectly with rhymes from
fellow Killa Beez: Ghostface
Killah, RZA, GZA, Method
Man, and Raekwon. Together
they created legendary
masterpieces.

V is for **V**anilla Ice.
He wasn't the most skilled
rapper, but Vanilla Ice owns
a piece of hip-hop history.
In 1990, the Iceman rocked
the mic like a vandal and
helped attract a wider
mainstream audience with
"Ice Ice Baby." It was the
first rap song to top the
pop charts.

W is for Kanye **West.**
This college dropout released tons of GOOD music in the 2000s, becoming arguably the best rapper of his generation. With more than 20 Grammys, Yeezy is a lyrical and musical genius who has made his mark on 21st century popular culture.

X is for DM**X**.
A rapper with a gruff, growling voice, DMX and his Ruff Ryder family were responsible for some legendary songs in the late '90s and early 2000s. Millions around the world partied to his tunes, with his first three major-label albums all debuting at No.1.

Yy

Y is for Adam **Y**auch. Better known as MCA, he was one of the legendary Beastie Boys. With a 'license to ill,' this groundbreaking trio of white rappers rewrote the rules, mixing rap and rock in the '80s to create a new style of music and help millions fight for their right to party.

Z is for JAY-Z.
H to the Izz-O, V to the
Izz-A! JAY-Z overcame his
hard knock life to become
hip-hop royalty. He set a
rapper record with his 22nd
Grammy Award in 2018.
He might have 99 problems,
but legendary status
ain't one!

The ever-expanding legendary library

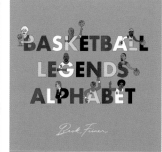

EXPLORE THESE LEGENDARY ALPHABETS & MORE AT WWW.ALPHABETLEGENDS.COM

HIP-HOP LEGENDS ALPHABET
www.alphabetlegends.com

Published by Alphabet Legends Pty Ltd in 2021
Created by Beck Feiner
Copyright © Alphabet Legends Pty Ltd 2021

9780645200133

Printed and bound in China.

ALPHABET LEGENDS